Recovery Manual

RECOVERY MANUAL

Poems by Penney Knightly

LBME Publishing

Recovery Manual
LBME Publishing LLC: http://LBMEPublishing.com/
ISBN: 978-1-64676-000-8 (trade paperback)
ISBN: 978-1-64676-001-5 (ebook)

First Edition

Printed in the United States of America.

To my men, who gave me hope.
You are the reason for everything.

Table of Contents

UPSETTING

The heavy hand of waking up
bites my lip and calls it good.
There is fighting at the back of my eyes
but everything is as calm as a cadaver.

It's really odd
when you punch out
the side of the apple cart
rolling down the hill and on
and you think *there is momentum*
what a force to be reckoned with
and you think of your hair as steady guides
keeping the rest of you covered like a curtain;

a snowfall.

THE NEW THERAPIST

Across, again. Two islands.
Mine is mostly uninhabited.
I settled for stalks and rain;
the tops of the trees are low,
oppressive as oil.

You have homes on yours,
lawns, care. Considerations
to keep: children swinging,
the carousel of management means
you actually have a purse
with an actual day book.

I talk at you,
more arms than I have
outstretched over years
and emotion, you gather
and pick and type and write
you snatch color and make tags,
you note as if it is your way of speaking
tongue scribbles, mummification
of what I was,
of what I say,
of what I really mean.

Extractions Are Not Hard

you just bite a little and take it

feeling like tackle is the point
when what penetrates is yourself

you just have to fake until
the dagger pulls out

then you can make it
a little while longer

if you hold your breath
it feels like flying

Timing

As you walk away,
time, being all that it is,
skips and hangs high
and strikes as lightning,
the ants move from point to point,
do you think there is a point
between where and there
how we're going so fast
but can't stop to feel,
as you pass this way
is a storm cell, as I dive into
the heaviness of your skin
I wait for sounds, but
it is what is always is.

In Which I Am Not All Good & You Are Not All Bad

I run around the back
poke my eyes through the holes your eyes
and see the sun
the razor of the moon splices hard
the grit of my teeth on your throat
I pass through you like rooms
your throat is a chimney,
tongue so loose it's melted

it wasn't so black and white
I wasn't a deer, spring step
scared bunny in dark leaves
smelling of bark and wet dead
hands on insides of skirts and sea
going down two large legs
salty corners of mouths
the slip into one another
like a falling star, black hole hunger
there was smoke and craters and hell
you were willing, so I stepped in.

Recovery Manual

When I turn to the bottle,
I am only drinking.

When I cry in my sleep,
I am running.

When I wail in the night,
I am singing.

When age caves my eyes in,
I am remembering.

When hope is done,
I am enduring.

When badness is there,
I am lying.

When I turn to rest,
I am still here.

The Ocean Is a Loss

Such heaviness and incomplete
surrounding and moving
making waves as it were.

Salt-teared, so much going on
shriveled under trees shadowed lips
on edges, dirty climbs and mud-swallowed,
embankments of tender and fallen
everything comes in.

Ache in darkness, mild quiet
bridges and illuminations, shuddered thunder
caps of white rimmed in sun-glare,
tints of heaven with wrinkled woes
so animalistic, debris of fallen wars,
ships, blood, and continuation—

A ravage with heat, a cold crush with ice,
burns and pushes, wind-to-your-back,
my eyes are on you.

Your weight is life,
you carry moon and tide and fish and feel;
the anchor of what you are
is motion.

THE MOST FUNCTIONAL PRAYER

A footstep is taken, *hallelujah*.
We eat butter and bread and there is ice.

Snow is for beautifying and isn't taking toes.
My legs work and cross and open.

I can take your tongue like a burning lantern.
I can make you in my image and we will not die.

There is laughter and crying,
my mother is still in the room, not in the ground,
there is lavender to smell and sheets and pillows.

Lines on my face still count as character.
I raise a glass, I can swallow.

The marvel of eyes sees and accepts.

Time brings bright light to blue-mooned night.
There is anger but it dies with sleep.

Memory Fruit

Heart is craggy and well-worn,
I ate every hour and it was filled
with time and space and insects
the size of apples, with fire.

I dove off the back porch.
You wouldn't have known it;
you were too busy kissing her downstairs.

The foyer that divides her was split and hot
and you had to use the extinguisher
of your tongue.

There are always those lanterns in the sky.
I count them like lullabies,
I see the wind and it sees back.

I like the roll of ground and air
on my back, everything good I know
happens in this position.

Organic

means skin as real as a baby I saw
roasting on the grill
maddened mass of scream
smoke, it was there
and it wasn't there
and it was there

at the table there is white flesh
it is chicken cluck pluck feathered
once, bare as bones found in riverbeds
as bright and blinding as my neck
when you wrapped the white rope
around and make me choke for laughs,
which was good because I need those
humor, dark and black and mossy,
coffee-colored like dried blood,
I need that, too

I think of the source
making it become small pieces
it goes in me in slow bites and doesn't get to come
back out, it doesn't get to come
back in, it doesn't get to come

under the fluorescent lights in the aisle
of the place where we buy meat,
you buy me wholesale knowing everything

twine and back legged, slow submission I simmer in
knives and butter and spice and force
I know you, I know this.
I know.

Let me hold back
it feels like nothing,
sandbags on my veins,
anticipating rains, the rush of volumes,
the hectic catch of what could come.

I eat bags. Stuff them down my throat.
You never know what you're going to keep
and what will keep you going. The ache
is pulse throbbing in my eyelids like a snakebite;
my lips are so stoic and statuesque, sometimes
the idea of words starts small scars.

Busy beavers of my thoughts
patching, scratching, tending;
they cannot imagine endangerment,
they hide in nests they build themselves.

My hair strands are loose and cursing,
don't want to be attached. Set free
they would walk like lions, through
the jungle of the wind.

BLUEPRINT

Someone described each stanza as a room
and I believe it is.
Where else can you make space
and redecorate so quickly?

I like to keep it simple,
flat, holding, and only
what has to be.
It doesn't remind me of anything;
it is not pretentious like that.

Fully-furnished isn't wrong,
it is just another way;
the vases already filled with tears
make it easier to break.

I don't believe in carpet—
too much work to get out blood.
I would rather spend that time with you
in buckets, on my knees.

Equally

I believe in keeping the small choices:
her choice of gum, the meatloaf recipe
with brown sugar and ketchup,
the small teachings
of how to shuck corn, how to smack
an iceberg lettuce onto a table
letting the inside out, what it feels like
to be given a job: tiny hands in iron-smelling beef
making dinner for a household of six,
the smell of onion, and the crying that came with
foods stuck on walls from flying plates,
helplessness of a child, being told
she wishes you were never born. And how
you don't even remember what that was about
but you remember the words and the look in her eyes.
She meant all of this.
Equally.

What is the line of love and hate?
How can you know? Does it make a noise
when you crossover? There must be a warning.
Coming back may be possible.

Or are they one and the same?

After Party

Half undone, sides of my dress sleeves sliding,
I remind myself of so many Hollywood harlots.
I am housemaid Monroe, a non-vampish intermediary,

with nowhere to go,
small little party of one,
lonely as a soft, round flower in a vase,
containment, contrived elegance.

But quiet rapture happens, in the brain,
the moan of ecstasy engulfing:
like that time I was on the phone with my mother
and you went down like a tropic sunset,
bursts of waves between phrases

alone, aware of sex spreading out
onto the room like a carpet over ground,
or a rush of ivy over the fence;
wavelengths between dust, flavors of air,
melted honey, bees of sting and sweating pain,
a wet musk of youth, sitting ignition.

Recline, a brief thought of self-satisfaction in the middle:
Plan B, an escape, a weaker extract, yet self-tested, exact.

Before going off, a short love letter:
to all my children that have not been born,
all the love that was lost, long imagined from before,
the tilt of the slip, the slit between the hips,

flower petals bloom in pocketed places,
the dress holds heart, skin, and breast
akin to arrest.

FLAME TO PAPER

the past is a dollhouse
looks like everything that used to be
shapes and small rooms
it looks real

somehow in some way
you happened to bite like Alice
and get big
and walk the fuck out

of those divided glue
and paper rooms
that don't support
any weight

you could easily take a match
light it up like
all those Christmas trees
between your legs
you could do it

A Black Opus

I.
I could be a constellation.
I have a cryptic, enticing tale,
with lions and swords
and those things,
blood and love
and choices of kings.

II.
I am entirely
stitched together
as a black opus,
low-hanging stars
as shimmer fruits,
tasting time in the forest,
the apple butter of my experience
is ravage, is pitted, pulled from.

III.
The language of your hair,
the bristles of your eyes,
the savage of the skin,
in the mirror-glass-tongue of water,
the hunger in your fingers,
the lamentation in your groin,
the bleeding of your ears,
the words are softened with oil.

IV.
I am prune-like. Been in too long.
I have courage like a walking stick.
I lean, I temper, I cry:
this is the art of standing.

Unconscious is Not Good Enough

for temporary relief there is sleep
but I'm full of it & wander past
lights that live here are not real
I have not seen a photon worth my time
there is courage in keeping going but it's labor
to convince your skin to stay on you have to work
on opening your eyes really far really wide really really
seriously
if you let go for just one one one second the heart will
catch on and kill us

The Secret War of Restraint

what do you do when
you want to be the other woman
but not really, just sort of
take him for a ride and let
him have it, you know
that sort of thing, where
you bite, make him pay,
talk as dirty as your unfiltered mind

what happens
when the reality of reality
doesn't hold the image all the well
and you think it's a good idea to step
over the line, and hell, what line
I didn't even notice a bump in the road
I couldn't have possibly hit anything

where do you go
with the dark underside, the one
that makes objects out of breathing people
and you think they can all fill
and you will buy orifices as needed
and it will all be clay and rock and anger
and you can cut mash burn grind bleed
& it will feel like everything
and nothing ever could

Object Lesson from Nature

I picked up dirt.
It was more than me—
ground and particulate,
fine and blowing, chalky
as a lung in a dust bowl.

It looked desaturated,
as light as milk,
crispy, cool as death
ageless because it is depth,
not because it has eyes.

I see a jump in the brush,
a sage little fellow,
blue as a vein,
two tiny legs to carry it.

How it picks
at the rocks and earth,
how it makes a nest
from what has fallen.

I Want to Know the Ending

It's not as if I don't want to,
because I do.
If you were to ask, I'd say
I'm tired of all the time.
This isn't me wishing I were older
or saying I am done living,
or anything like that.

I just feel like going faster,
through the moves a little quicker.
In the movies I'd get a montage,
the way it so romantically portrays,
devoid of struggle and emotion.

I suppose it is impatience,
the unwillingness to wait for inevitability.
Slow turnover makes me scared.

I like the peace that comes from seeing
an aging woman's body;
she withstands.

Acknowledgments

"Recovery Manual"
— published in <u>Awakened Voices</u>

"Memory Fruit"
— first appeared on <u>Virtual Verse</u>

"After Party"
— published in <u>Broad Magazine</u>

"Object Lesson from Nature"
— first appeared on <u>Anti-Heroin Chic</u>

"A Black Opus"
— first appeared on <u>Cleaver Magazine</u>

"I Want to Know the Ending"
— published in <u>Gold Man Review</u>

A Note From the Author

Dear Reader,

This book is independently published. I depend on your reviews and word-of-mouth.

If you enjoy this book, please help spread the word through various social media. Please consider also writing a review on Amazon.com or Goodreads.com, or your favorite venue.

Thanks for purchasing the book. I hope you enjoy it.

Penney Knightly
California Coast, 2019

About the Author

Penney Knightly is a poet and artist. She is a survivor of many years of intense physical, emotional, mental, and sexual abuse, themes that are often found in her work.

For many years, she used poetry and art to assist in her recovery from depression and dissociation. Today, many victims of abuse, their relatives, and friends find comfort, understanding, and inspiration in her poems.

Her poetry has appeared in Anti-Heroin Chic, Cleaver, Dead King, Ink in Thirds, Burningword Journal, and elsewhere.

She lives with her family on a sailboat on the San Francisco Bay. She tweets @penneyknightly and can be found online at http://penneyknightly.com.

www.ingramcontent.com/pod-product-compliance
Lightning Source LLC
Chambersburg PA
CBHW020350110726
47898CB00003B/1103